SCHOLASTIC

D1384830

SUPER SUDOKU MATH

ADDITION & SUBTRACTION FACTS

Eric Charlesworth

To Henry "Hammerin' Hank" Cole—E. C.

Editor: Sarah Longhi
Cover designer: Jason Robinson
Interior designer: Kelli Thompson
Illustrator: Teresa Anderko

ISBN-13: 978-0-545-17457-2
ISBN-10: 0-545-17457-0

1 2 3 4 5 6 7 8 9 10   40   16 15 14 13 12 11 10

New York • Toronto • London • Auckland • Sydney
Mexico City • New Delhi • Hong Kong • Buenos Aires

Teaching *Resources*

Contents

Introduction

Welcome to a new type of math practice that will engage students of all levels while reinforcing critical skills for math success!

As a middle-school math teacher, I see firsthand how students who are unable to do basic operations quickly encounter serious challenges with more sophisticated math work. Students who have trouble with automaticity tend to get overwhelmed by the more demanding (and more interesting) concepts and problem solving they face in middle school. It is no wonder that so many of these students harbor negative attitudes toward math as they realize the importance of the skills they lack. I work with students to help them overcome these difficulties in my classroom, using puzzles and games like the ones in this book. I'm eager to share these tools so that we can better support struggling students before they arrive in middle school.

In its Standards & Focal Points document (2006), the National Council of Teachers of Mathematics advises that students gain computational fluency with addition and subtraction in the primary grades. This book is designed to provide the type of engaging work with repeated practice that helps students achieve mastery. You can replace most rote facts-practice worksheets with the 41 leveled Sudoku puzzle challenges in this collection. Here are some key advantages to using these puzzles:

1 They promote algebraic reasoning and build understanding of the inverse relationship between addition and subtraction.

$18 - \_\_\_ = 12$ is just one step away from $18 - y = 12$.

2 They provide multiple pathways to finding the right answer, which supports flexible thinking.

3 They encourage students to use trial-and-error and deductive reasoning to find the solution, thus building problem-solving skills while supporting automaticity with basic facts.

4 The puzzles are self-checking. Students feel empowered when they do them. If everything comes out right, they feel good. If they make an error, they will quickly find that the puzzle isn't working, which will help them catch the mistake and try to correct it themselves.

5 Students who have struggled with rote, repetitive sheets are tired of them. The more advanced students, who breeze through those sheets, are also sick of them. With this book, all students get a new window into facts practice.

Facts are Fun!

Regular-sized puzzle

9 +_ = 10	8 +4 = 1_	11 +3 = 1_	5 +_ = 8
3 +_ = 6	_ +3 = 7	9 +3 = 1_	7 +4 = 1_
0 +2 = _	10 +_ = 13	9 +2 = _1	1 +3 = _
6 +_ = 10	10 +_ = 11	9 +4 = 1_	6 +_ = 8

Regular-sized puzzle

Super-sized puzzle

_ +1 = 7	_ +2 = 7	7 +_ = 10	12 +2 = 1_	7 +4 = 1_	10 +_ = 12
1 +_ = 2	6 +_ = 8	8 +_ = 12	_ +3 = 8	_ +4 = 10	10 +_ = 13
0 +_ = 3	4 +_ = 8	3 +2 = _	_ +2 = 8	9 +_ = 11	10 +1 = 1_
11 +_ = 13	0 +_ = 1	_ +3 = 9	11 +2 = 1_	3 +_ = 7	4 +1 = _
8 +_ = 12	4 +_ = 7	7 +_ = 9	11 +_ = 12	_ +4 = 9	12 +4 = 1_
11 +4 = 1_	5 +1 = _	6 +_ = 7	8 +_ = 10	9 +4 = 1_	2 +_ = 6

Super-sized puzzle

How to Use This Book

These puzzles can be used flexibly. You may want to hand out copies of the puzzles for a warm-up activity (or "do now") to start class. However, they can also be given to students who finish their class work early or occasionally as homework.

Best of all, it is easy to differentiate with this book.

The super-sized Sudoku puzzles (6-by-6 grids) are more complex than the regular-sized puzzles (4-by-4 grids) and can be given to students who are ready for the challenge. Here are some additional ways to meet the needs of the diverse learners in your classroom.

Challenge activities:

- Have students solve the Word Problems that appear at the bottom of some of the puzzle pages.
- Time students to see how quickly they can complete the puzzles—and beat their own best times. (Make sure this is done in a non-competitive, non-public way.)
- Have students create their own Sudoku puzzle to give to their classmates. Once they are familiar with the format, some students will love doing this.

Ways to support struggling students:

- Have them practice with easy-level standard Sudoku puzzles first to build their confidence with the format.
- Model or solve puzzles as a class on the overhead or the interactive whiteboard.
- Allow students to refer to the Addition and Subtraction Tables on page 5. (You may enlarge the tables as needed.)
- Use the tips included at the bottom of some of the Sudoku puzzle pages.

Another way to differentiate is to allow some students practice with the puzzles in this book while students who are more secure with these facts try puzzles from the companion books, *Super Sudoku Math: Multiplication & Division Facts* and *Super Sudoku Math: Fractions & Decimals*.

NCTM Standard Connection

Students develop fluency with basic number combinations for addition and subtraction (fact families 1–10).

Addition Table

+	0	1	2	3	4	5	6	7	8	9	10	11	12
0	0	1	2	3	4	5	6	7	8	9	10	11	12
1	1	2	3	4	5	6	7	8	9	10	11	12	13
2	2	3	4	5	6	7	8	9	10	11	12	13	14
3	3	4	5	6	7	8	9	10	11	12	13	14	15
4	4	5	6	7	8	9	10	11	12	13	14	15	16
5	5	6	7	8	9	10	11	12	13	14	15	16	17
6	6	7	8	9	10	11	12	13	14	15	16	17	18
7	7	8	9	10	11	12	13	14	15	16	17	18	19
8	8	9	10	11	12	13	14	15	16	17	18	19	20
9	9	10	11	12	13	14	15	16	17	18	19	20	21
10	10	11	12	13	14	15	16	17	18	19	20	21	22
11	11	12	13	14	15	16	17	18	19	20	21	22	23
12	12	13	14	15	16	17	18	19	20	21	22	23	24

How to use this table

Example: To find **8 + 3**:

1. Go down to the **"8"** row.   **2.** Follow the **"8"** row across to meet the **"3"** column.   **3.** Find your answer: **11**!

Subtraction Table

–	1	2	3	4	5	6	7	8	9	10	11	12
1	0	–	–	–	–	–	–	–	–	–	–	–
2	1	0	–	–	–	–	–	–	–	–	–	–
3	2	1	0	–	–	–	–	–	–	–	–	–
4	3	2	1	0	–	–	–	–	–	–	–	–
5	4	3	2	1	0	–	–	–	–	–	–	–
6	5	4	3	2	1	0	–	–	–	–	–	–
7	6	5	4	3	2	1	0	–	–	–	–	–
8	7	6	5	4	3	2	1	0	–	–	–	–
9	8	7	6	5	4	3	2	1	0	–	–	–
10	9	8	7	6	5	4	3	2	1	0	–	–
11	10	9	8	7	6	5	4	3	2	1	0	–
12	11	10	9	8	7	6	5	4	3	2	1	0
13	12	11	10	9	8	7	6	5	4	3	2	1
14	13	12	11	10	9	8	7	6	5	4	3	2
15	14	13	12	11	10	9	8	7	6	5	4	3
16	15	14	13	12	11	10	9	8	7	6	5	4
17	16	15	14	13	12	11	10	9	8	7	6	5
18	17	16	15	14	13	12	11	10	9	8	7	6
19	18	17	16	15	14	13	12	11	10	9	8	7
20	19	18	17	16	15	14	13	12	11	10	9	8
21	20	19	18	17	16	15	14	13	12	11	10	9
22	21	20	19	18	17	16	15	14	13	12	11	10
23	22	21	20	19	18	17	16	15	14	13	12	11
24	23	22	21	20	19	18	17	16	15	14	13	12

How to use this table

Example: To find **12 – 4**:

1. Go down to the **"12"** row.   **2.** Follow the **"12"** row across to meet the **"4"** column.   **3.** Find your answer: **8**!

Super SUDOKU RULES

Regular-sized Puzzles

Rule 1

1	2	3	4
3	4	1	2
2	1	4	3
4	3	2	1

▶ Fill in the **row** so that it contains numbers 1 through 4.

Rule 2

1	2	3	4
3	4	1	2
2	1	4	3
4	3	2	1

▶ Fill in the **column** so that it contains numbers 1 through 4.

Rule 3

1	2	3	4
3	4	1	2
2	1	4	3
4	3	2	1

▶ Fill in the 2-by-2 **box** so that it contains the numbers 1 through 4.

Super-sized Puzzles

1	2	3	4	5	6
3	4	1	2	6	5
2	1	5	3	4	6
4	5	6	1	2	3
6	2	4	5	1	3
2	5	1	4	3	6

▶ Fill in the **row** so that it contains numbers 1 through 6.

1	2	3	4	5	6
2	4	1	2	6	5
3	1	5	3	4	6
4	5	6	1	2	3
5	2	4	5	1	3
6	5	1	4	3	6

▶ Fill in the **column** so that it contains numbers 1 through 6.

1	2	3	4	5	6
4	5	6	2	6	5
2	1	5	3	4	6
4	5	6	1	2	3
6	2	4	5	1	3
2	5	1	4	3	6

▶ Fill in the 3-by-2 **box** so that it contains the numbers 1 through 6.

TIP!

For many of the regular-sized puzzles in this book, you will fill in the spaces with the numbers 5, 6, 7 and 8 instead of 1, 2, 3 and 4. All other rules remain the same.

Super Sudoku Math: Addition & Subtraction Facts • © 2010 by Eric Charlesworth • Scholastic Teaching Resources

Super SUDOKU

Name _____ Date _____

Adding With 1 and 2

Directions

● Every row, column, and 2-by-2 box ⊞ should contain each of these digits:

5   6   7   8

● Fill in each blank with the correct number to complete the fact.

‾ + 1 —— 6	‾ + 2 —— 9	7 + 1 —— ‾	‾ + 1 —— 7
‾ + 2 —— 8	‾ + 1 —— 9	‾ + 2 —— 7	5 + 2 —— ‾
6 + 1 —— ‾	4 + 1 —— ‾	‾ + 1 —— 7	6 + 2 —— ‾
‾ + 2 —— 10	4 + 2 —— ‾	‾ + 2 —— 9	3 + 2 —— ‾

Tip!

Adding 1 to a number is just like counting. Just say the next number and that's your answer!

Name _____ Date _____

Adding With **3** and **4**

Directions

● Every row, column, and 2-by-2 box ⊞ should contain each of these digits:

1   **2**   **3**   **4**

● Fill in each blank with the correct number to complete the fact.

11 + 3 ――― 1_	8 + 4 ――― 1_	_ + 3 ――― 4	3 + _ ――― 6
7 + 4 ――― 1_	7 + _ ――― 10	3 + _ ――― 7	_ + 4 ――― 6
6 + _ ――― 9	8 + 3 ――― 1_	9 + 3 ――― 1_	9 + _ ――― 13
_ + 3 ――― 5	6 + _ ――― 10	5 + _ ――― 8	_ + 4 ――― 5

Tip!

The first facts to memorize are the doubles
(1 + 1 = 2, 2 + 2 = 4, 3 + 3 = 6, and so on). Doubles
can help you remember other facts. For example,
5 + 5 = 10 so 5 + 4 is just one less... 9.

Super Sudoku Math: Addition & Subtraction Facts • © 2010 by Eric Charlesworth • Scholastic Teaching Resources

Name _____ Date _____

Adding With **1, 2, 3,** and **4**

Directions

● Every row, column, and 2-by-2 box ⊞ should contain each of these digits:

1 **2** **3** **4**

● Fill in each blank with the correct number to complete the fact.

9 + _ 10	8 + 4 1_	11 + 3 1_	5 + _ 8
3 + _ 6	_ + 3 7	9 + 3 1_	7 + 4 1_
0 + 2 _	10 + _ 13	9 + 2 _1	1 + 3 _
6 + _ 10	10 + _ 11	9 + 4 1_	6 + _ 8

Tip!

The answer to an addition problem is called a *sum*. The sum of 2 and 3 is 5. What's the sum of 4 and 3?

_____

9

Name _____ Date _____

Adding With **1, 2, 3,** and **4**

Directions

● Every row, column, and 2-by-2 box ⊞ should contain each of these digits:

5 **6** **7** **8**

● Fill in each blank with the correct number to complete the fact.

___ + 4 11	11 + 4 1__	12 + 4 1__	___ + 1 9
___ + 3 9	4 + 4	___ + 3 10	12 + 3 1__
___ + 3 8	5 + 1	5 + 3	___ + 2 9
___ + 2 10	___ + 1 8	___ + 1 6	4 + 2

Word Problem

Christiana has four pens on her desk, four pens in her cubby, and four pens in her backpack. How many pens does she have in all?

_____

Super Sudoku Math: Addition & Subtraction Facts • © 2010 by Eric Charlesworth • Scholastic Teaching Resources

Super SUDOKU

Name _____ Date _____

Adding With 1, 2, 3, and 4

Directions

● Every row, column, and 3-by-2 box [grid] should contain each of these digits:

1 2 3 4 5 6

● Fill in each blank with the correct number to complete the fact.

7 + _ —— 9	10 + _ —— 14	8 + _ —— 11	2 + _ —— 3	3 + 2 ——	4 + 2 ——
12 + 3 —— 1_	7 + _ —— 8	_ + 4 —— 10	6 + _ —— 9	8 + 4 —— 1_	12 + 2 —— 1_
12 + 1 —— 1_	8 + _ —— 10	8 + _ —— 9	8 + _ —— 12	_ + 2 —— 8	_ + 1 —— 6
4 + _ —— 8	12 + 4 —— 1_	_ + 2 —— 7	4 + _ —— 6	9 + 4 —— 1_	10 + 1 —— 1_
3 + 3 ——	9 + _ —— 12	5 + _ —— 9	1 + 4 ——	7 + 4 —— 1_	9 + 3 —— 1_
0 + _ —— 1	11 + 4 —— 1_	11 + _ —— 13	_ + 2 —— 8	11 + 3 —— 1_	5 + _ —— 8

Name _____ Date _____

Adding With **1, 2, 3,** and **4**

Directions

● Every row, column, and 3-by-2 box ⊞ should contain each of these digits:

1   **2**   **3**   **4**   **5**   **6**

● Fill in each blank with the correct number to complete the fact.

$\begin{array}{r}\_\\ +\,1\\ \hline 7\end{array}$	$\begin{array}{r}\_\\ +\,2\\ \hline 7\end{array}$	$\begin{array}{r}7\\ +\,\_\\ \hline 10\end{array}$	$\begin{array}{r}12\\ +\,2\\ \hline 1\_\end{array}$	$\begin{array}{r}7\\ +\,4\\ \hline 1\_\end{array}$	$\begin{array}{r}10\\ +\,\_\\ \hline 12\end{array}$
$\begin{array}{r}1\\ +\,\_\\ \hline 2\end{array}$	$\begin{array}{r}6\\ +\,\_\\ \hline 8\end{array}$	$\begin{array}{r}8\\ +\,\_\\ \hline 12\end{array}$	$\begin{array}{r}\_\\ +\,3\\ \hline 8\end{array}$	$\begin{array}{r}\_\\ +\,4\\ \hline 10\end{array}$	$\begin{array}{r}10\\ +\,\_\\ \hline 13\end{array}$
$\begin{array}{r}0\\ +\,\_\\ \hline 3\end{array}$	$\begin{array}{r}4\\ +\,\_\\ \hline 8\end{array}$	$\begin{array}{r}3\\ +\,2\\ \hline \_\end{array}$	$\begin{array}{r}\_\\ +\,2\\ \hline 8\end{array}$	$\begin{array}{r}9\\ +\,\_\\ \hline 11\end{array}$	$\begin{array}{r}10\\ +\,1\\ \hline 1\_\end{array}$
$\begin{array}{r}11\\ +\,\_\\ \hline 13\end{array}$	$\begin{array}{r}0\\ +\,\_\\ \hline 1\end{array}$	$\begin{array}{r}\_\\ +\,3\\ \hline 9\end{array}$	$\begin{array}{r}11\\ +\,2\\ \hline 1\_\end{array}$	$\begin{array}{r}3\\ +\,\_\\ \hline 7\end{array}$	$\begin{array}{r}4\\ +\,1\\ \hline \_\end{array}$
$\begin{array}{r}8\\ +\,\_\\ \hline 12\end{array}$	$\begin{array}{r}4\\ +\,\_\\ \hline 7\end{array}$	$\begin{array}{r}7\\ +\,\_\\ \hline 9\end{array}$	$\begin{array}{r}11\\ +\,\_\\ \hline 12\end{array}$	$\begin{array}{r}\_\\ +\,4\\ \hline 9\end{array}$	$\begin{array}{r}12\\ +\,4\\ \hline 1\_\end{array}$
$\begin{array}{r}11\\ +\,4\\ \hline 1\_\end{array}$	$\begin{array}{r}5\\ +\,1\\ \hline \_\end{array}$	$\begin{array}{r}6\\ +\,\_\\ \hline 7\end{array}$	$\begin{array}{r}8\\ +\,\_\\ \hline 10\end{array}$	$\begin{array}{r}9\\ +\,4\\ \hline 1\_\end{array}$	$\begin{array}{r}2\\ +\,\_\\ \hline 6\end{array}$

Super SUDOKU

Name _____ Date _____

Adding With 5 and 6

Directions

● Every row, column, and 2-by-2 box ⊞ should contain each of these digits:

5   6   7   8

● Fill in each blank with the correct number to complete the fact.

3 + _ —— 9	2 + 5 —— _	_ + 6 —— 14	4 + _ —— 9
8 + _ —— 13	2 + 6 —— _	1 + 6 —— _	10 + _ —— 16
12 + 5 —— 1_	9 + _ —— 14	7 + _ —— 13	3 + 5 —— _
12 + 6 —— 1_	6 + _ —— 12	10 + _ —— 15	11 + 6 —— 1_

Tip!

Make sure you know all the sums that equal 10. They are 1 + 9, 2 + 8, 3 + 7, 4 + 6, and 5 + 5. Knowing these will make it easier to solve lots of other math problems.

Super Sudoku Math: Addition & Subtraction Facts • © 2010 by Eric Charlesworth • Scholastic Teaching Resources

Name _____ Date _____

Adding With 7 and 8

Directions

● Every row, column, and 2-by-2 box ⊞ should contain each of these digits:

5   6   7   8

● Fill in each blank with the correct number to complete the fact.

2 + _ ___ 9	3 + _ ___ 11	8 + 7 ___ 1_	9 + 7 ___ 1_
_ + 7 ___ 12	_ + 7 ___ 13	9 + _ ___ 17	11 + _ ___ 18
8 + 8 ___ 1_	7 + 8 ___ 1_	7 + _ ___ 14	10 + 8 ___ 1_
4 + _ ___ 12	4 + _ ___ 11	_ + 8 ___ 14	_ + 8 ___ 13

Word Problem

Jeffrey read 3 pages of his book on Friday, 6 pages on Saturday, and 8 pages on Sunday. How many total pages did he read?

_____

Super Sudoku Math: Addition & Subtraction Facts • © 2010 by Eric Charlesworth • Scholastic Teaching Resources

Name _____ Date _____

Adding With **5, 6, 7,** and **8**

Directions

● Every row, column, and 2-by-2 box ⊞ should contain each of these digits:

1   **2**   **3**   **4**

● Fill in each blank with the correct number to complete the fact.

_ + 7 8	12 + 8 _0	7 + 7 1_	7 + 6 1_
_ + 6 9	_ + 6 10	7 + 5 1_	_ + 8 9
6 + 6 1_	8 + _ 11	6 + 5 1_	8 + 6 1_
_ + 5 9	1_ + 7 18	_ + 7 10	_ + 8 10

Word Problem

Alex has 7 apples and one fewer banana than he has apples. How many pieces of fruit does he have in all?

_____

Name _____ Date _____

Adding With **5, 6, 7,** and **8**

Directions

● Every row, column, and 2-by-2 box ⊞ should contain each of these digits:

5   **6**   **7**   **8**

● Fill in each blank with the correct number to complete the fact.

‾ + 4 —— 11	11 + 4 —— 1_	12 + 4 —— 1_	‾ + 1 —— 9
‾ + 3 —— 9	4 + 4 ——	‾ + 3 —— 10	12 + 3 —— 1_
‾ + 3 —— 8	5 + 1 ——	5 + 3 ——	‾ + 2 —— 9
‾ + 2 —— 10	‾ + 1 —— 8	‾ + 1 —— 6	4 + 2 ——

Word Problem

Eliza has $6 and her sister Elaine has $5. Do they have enough money to buy a puzzle that costs $8?

_____

Super SUDOKU

Name _____   Date _____

Adding With **1–8**

Directions

● Every row, column, and 3-by-2 box ⊞ should contain each of these digits:

1   2   3   4   5   6

● Fill in each blank with the correct number to complete the fact.

$\begin{array}{r} \underline{} \\ +\,7 \\ \hline 10 \end{array}$	$\begin{array}{r} 10 \\ +\,\underline{} \\ \hline 12 \end{array}$	$\begin{array}{r} 7 \\ +\,7 \\ \hline 1\underline{} \end{array}$	$\begin{array}{r} 8 \\ +\,8 \\ \hline 1\underline{} \end{array}$	$\begin{array}{r} \underline{}1 \\ +\,7 \\ \hline 18 \end{array}$	$\begin{array}{r} 0 \\ +\,\underline{} \\ \hline 5 \end{array}$
$\begin{array}{r} 3 \\ +\,3 \\ \hline \end{array}$	$\begin{array}{r} \underline{} \\ +\,7 \\ \hline 12 \end{array}$	$\begin{array}{r} 7 \\ +\,4 \\ \hline 1\underline{} \end{array}$	$\begin{array}{r} 0 \\ +\,3 \\ \hline \end{array}$	$\begin{array}{r} 11 \\ +\,\underline{} \\ \hline 15 \end{array}$	$\begin{array}{r} 8 \\ +\,4 \\ \hline 1\underline{} \end{array}$
$\begin{array}{r} 6 \\ +\,6 \\ \hline 1\underline{} \end{array}$	$\begin{array}{r} \underline{} \\ +\,8 \\ \hline 12 \end{array}$	$\begin{array}{r} 12 \\ +\,4 \\ \hline 1\underline{} \end{array}$	$\begin{array}{r} \underline{} \\ +\,5 \\ \hline 10 \end{array}$	$\begin{array}{r} 8 \\ +\,5 \\ \hline 1\underline{} \end{array}$	$\begin{array}{r} \underline{} \\ +\,4 \\ \hline 5 \end{array}$
$\begin{array}{r} 8 \\ +\,\underline{} \\ \hline 9 \end{array}$	$\begin{array}{r} 4 \\ +\,\underline{} \\ \hline 7 \end{array}$	$\begin{array}{r} 4 \\ +\,\underline{} \\ \hline 9 \end{array}$	$\begin{array}{r} \underline{} \\ +\,3 \\ \hline 5 \end{array}$	$\begin{array}{r} 11 \\ +\,5 \\ \hline 1\underline{} \end{array}$	$\begin{array}{r} 9 \\ +\,5 \\ \hline 1\underline{} \end{array}$
$\begin{array}{r} 10 \\ +\,\underline{} \\ \hline 15 \end{array}$	$\begin{array}{r} 10 \\ +\,\underline{} \\ \hline 11 \end{array}$	$\begin{array}{r} 10 \\ +\,\underline{} \\ \hline 13 \end{array}$	$\begin{array}{r} 4 \\ +\,\underline{} \\ \hline 8 \end{array}$	$\begin{array}{r} 1\underline{} \\ +\,4 \\ \hline 16 \end{array}$	$\begin{array}{r} 3 \\ +\,\underline{} \\ \hline 9 \end{array}$
$\begin{array}{r} \underline{} \\ +\,6 \\ \hline 10 \end{array}$	$\begin{array}{r} 5 \\ +\,\underline{} \\ \hline 11 \end{array}$	$\begin{array}{r} 7 \\ +\,\underline{} \\ \hline 9 \end{array}$	$\begin{array}{r} 9 \\ +\,6 \\ \hline \underline{}5 \end{array}$	$\begin{array}{r} 7 \\ +\,8 \\ \hline 1\underline{} \end{array}$	$\begin{array}{r} 7 \\ +\,6 \\ \hline 1\underline{} \end{array}$

Super SUDOKU

Name _____ Date _____

Adding With 1–8

Directions

● Every row, column, and 3-by-2 box ▦ should contain each of these digits:

1 2 3 4 5 6

● Fill in each blank with the correct number to complete the fact.

7 + _ 10	9 + _ 10	8 + 6 1_	7 + _ 13	4 + _ 6	2 + 3
6 + _ 8	5 + _ 10	3 + 3	10 + 4 1_	9 + _ 12	0 + 1
11 + _ 12	9 + 7 1_	3 + _ 5	0 + 5	9 + _ 13	_ + 4 7
_ + 6 10	8 + _ 11	1 + _ 6	1 + 1	9 + 2 1_	3 + _ 9
1 + _ 6	_ + 4 8	8 + 8 _6	10 + _ 13	5 + _ 11	7 + 5 1_
10 + 6 1_	_ + 8 10	12 + 1 1_	4 + 7 1_	12 + 3 1_	2 + _ 6

Super Sudoku Math: Addition & Subtraction Facts • © 2010 by Eric Charlesworth • Scholastic Teaching Resources

Name _____ Date _____

Adding With **9** and **10**

Directions

● Every row, column, and 2-by-2 box ⊞ should contain each of these digits:

5 **6** **7** **8**

● Fill in each blank with the correct number to complete the fact.

$\begin{array}{r}\underline{}\\ +\ 9\\ \hline 16\end{array}$	$\begin{array}{r}6\\ +\ 9\\ \hline 1\underline{}\end{array}$	$\begin{array}{r}6\\ +10\\ \hline 1\underline{}\end{array}$	$\begin{array}{r}\underline{}\\ +10\\ \hline 18\end{array}$
$\begin{array}{r}\underline{}\\ +\ 9\\ \hline 17\end{array}$	$\begin{array}{r}\underline{}\\ +10\\ \hline 16\end{array}$	$\begin{array}{r}\underline{}\\ +10\\ \hline 17\end{array}$	$\begin{array}{r}\underline{}\\ +\ 9\\ \hline 14\end{array}$
$\begin{array}{r}\underline{}\\ +10\\ \hline 15\end{array}$	$\begin{array}{r}7\\ +10\\ \hline 1\underline{}\end{array}$	$\begin{array}{r}9\\ +\ 9\\ \hline 1\underline{}\end{array}$	$\begin{array}{r}\underline{}\\ +\ 9\\ \hline 15\end{array}$
$\begin{array}{r}7\\ +\ 9\\ \hline 1\underline{}\end{array}$	$\begin{array}{r}8\\ +10\\ \hline 1\underline{}\end{array}$	$\begin{array}{r}5\\ +10\\ \hline 1\underline{}\end{array}$	$\begin{array}{r}8\\ +\ 9\\ \hline 1\underline{}\end{array}$

Tip!

Adding 10 to any number is easy.
Just add 1 in the tens place! For example:
7 + 10 = 17. 24 + 10 = 34. What is 76 + 10?

_____

Super SUDOKU

Name _____ Date _____

Adding With **11** and **12**

Directions

● Every row, column, and 2-by-2 box ⊞ should contain each of these digits:

1   **2**   **3**   **4**

● Fill in each blank with the correct number to complete the fact.

4 +1_ ――― 15	11 +12 ――― 2_	_ + 11 ――― 15	0 +1_ ――― 12
1 +11 ――― 1_	12 +12 ――― 2_	10 +11 ――― 2_	1 +12 ――― 1_
_ + 11 ――― 14	6 +_2 ――― 18	_ + 11 ――― 13	3 +11 ――― 1_
_ + 12 ――― 16	7 +1_ ――― 19	_ + 12 ――― 15	9 +12 ――― 2_

Word Problem

Teddy caught 5 fireflies each day two days in a row. On the third day he caught 11 more fireflies. How many fireflies did he catch in all?

_____

Super Sudoku Math: Addition & Subtraction Facts • © 2010 by Eric Charlesworth • Scholastic Teaching Resources

Name _____ Date _____

Adding With **9, 10, 11,** and **12**

Directions

● Every row, column, and 2-by-2 box ⊞ should contain each of these digits:

| 1 | 2 | 3 | 4 |

● Fill in each blank with the correct number to complete the fact.

12 + 9 — 2_	_ + 11 — 14	_ + 11 — 15	8 +12 — _0
_ + 12 — 14	5 + 9 — 1_	6 +_2 — 18	_ + 12 — 15
_ + 10 — 13	10 +11 — 2_	11 +11 — 2_	_ + 9 — 13
4 +10 — 1_	3 + 9 — 1_	_ + 9 — 12	_ + 9 — 10

Tip!

Adding 9 to a number is a snap.
First add 10 and then take back 1.
For example, for 9 + 9, think: *8 + 10*
(which is 18) and then take back 1
so your answer is 17.

Super SUDOKU

Name _____ Date _____

Adding With **9, 10, 11,** and **12**

Directions

● Every row, column, and 2-by-2 box ⊞ should contain each of these digits:

5   **6**   **7**   **8**

● Fill in each blank with the correct number to complete the fact.

‾ + 9 ───── 16	‾ + 12 ───── 20	‾ + 12 ───── 18	3 +12 ───── 1_
‾ + 9 ───── 14	7 + 9 ───── 1_	‾ + 11 ───── 19	6 +11 ───── 1_
9 + 9 ───── 1_	‾ + 10 ───── 15	‾ + 11 ───── 18	4 +12 ───── 1_
‾ + 10 ───── 16	5 +12 ───── 1_	6 + 9 ───── 1_	8 +10 ───── 1_

Word Problem

Annie made a block tower that was 12 blocks high. Then Justin added 10 more blocks to the tower. How many blocks high was the tower?

_____

Super Sudoku Math: Addition & Subtraction Facts • © 2010 by Eric Charlesworth • Scholastic Teaching Resources

Super SUDOKU

Name _____ Date _____

Adding With **1–12**

Directions

● Every row, column, and 3-by-2 box ⊞ should contain each of these digits:

| **1** | **2** | **3** | **4** | **5** | **6** |

● Fill in each blank with the correct number to complete the fact.

12 + 3 1_	2 + _ 4	1 + _ 4	3 + _ 7	4 + 7 1_	9 + _ 15
12 + 4 1_	7 + _ 8	0 + 4	7 + 6 1_	7 + _ 12	10 +12 2_
10 + _ 13	8 + _ 13	8 + 4 1_	9 +12 2_	11 + _ 17	2 + _ 6
2 + 2	11 + 5 1_	8 + _ 9	11 +11 2_	8 + _ 11	2 + _ 7
9 + 3 1_	4 + _ 7	8 + _ 14	7 + 8 1_	5 + _ 9	11 +10 2_
5 + 7 _2	11 + 3 1_	5 + _ 10	8 + 8 1_	_ + 7 9	7 + _ 10

Name _____ Date _____

Adding With 1–12

Directions

- Every row, column, and 3-by-2 box ⊞ should contain each of these digits:

  1 2 3 4 5 6

- Fill in each blank with the correct number to complete the fact.

6 + 6 1_	9 + 5 1_	7 + 8 1_	3 + 3	6 + _ 7	_ + 6 9
_ + 5 8	4 +12 1_	9 +12 2_	9 + _ 13	9 + _ 11	9 + _ 14
3 + 1	10 + 5 1_	9 + 3 1_	_ + 2 3	8 + 5 1_	0 + 6
9 + 7 1_	10 + 1 1_	_ + 3 6	6 + _ 11	6 + _ 10	8 +12 _0
3 +12 1_	5 + _ 7	12 + 2 1_	9 + 4 1_	11 + 5 1_	9 + _ 10
8 + 3 1_	_ + 2 5	5 + 1	10 + 2 1_	7 + _ 12	5 + _ 9

Super SUDOKU

Name _____ Date _____

Subtracting With **1** and **2**

Directions

● Every row, column, and 2-by-2 box ⊞ should contain each of these digits:

1 **2** **3** **4**

● Fill in each blank with the correct number to complete the fact.

5 − 2 ────	1_ − 2 ──── 12	9 − _ ──── 8	7 − _ ──── 5
8 − _ ──── 7	3 − _ ──── 1	5 − 1 ────	1_ − 2 ──── 11
10 − _ ──── 8	11 − _ ──── 10	4 − 1 ────	_ − 2 ──── 2
6 − 2 ────	1_ − 1 ──── 12	1_ − 2 ──── 10	1 − _ ──── 0

Tip!

Remember: If you add or subtract 0 from any number, the number stays the same! Zero doesn't change anything.

Name _____ Date _____

Subtracting With 3 and 4

Directions

- Every row, column, and 2-by-2 box ⊞ should contain each of these digits:

  1   2   3   4

- Fill in each blank with the correct number to complete the fact.

$\begin{array}{r} 1\_\_ \\ -\ 4 \\ \hline 7 \end{array}$	$\begin{array}{r} 1\_\_ \\ -\ 4 \\ \hline 8 \end{array}$	$\begin{array}{r} 12 \\ -\ \_\_ \\ \hline 9 \end{array}$	$\begin{array}{r} 7 \\ -\ 3 \\ \hline \end{array}$
$\begin{array}{r} 8 \\ -\ \_\_ \\ \hline 5 \end{array}$	$\begin{array}{r} 8 \\ -\ \_\_ \\ \hline 4 \end{array}$	$\begin{array}{r} 15 \\ -\ 3 \\ \hline 1\_\_ \end{array}$	$\begin{array}{r} 4 \\ -\ 3 \\ \hline \end{array}$
$\begin{array}{r} 10 \\ -\ \_\_ \\ \hline 6 \end{array}$	$\begin{array}{r} 9 \\ -\ \_\_ \\ \hline 6 \end{array}$	$\begin{array}{r} \_\_0 \\ -\ 3 \\ \hline 7 \end{array}$	$\begin{array}{r} 1\_\_ \\ -\ 3 \\ \hline 9 \end{array}$
$\begin{array}{r} 6 \\ -\ 4 \\ \hline \end{array}$	$\begin{array}{r} 5 \\ -\ 4 \\ \hline \end{array}$	$\begin{array}{r} 7 \\ -\ \_\_ \\ \hline 3 \end{array}$	$\begin{array}{r} 3 \\ -\ \_\_ \\ \hline 0 \end{array}$

Word Problem

Julia had 16 grapes but then she ate 4 of them. How many grapes does she have left?

_____

Super Sudoku Math: Addition & Subtraction Facts • © 2010 by Eric Charlesworth • Scholastic Teaching Resources

Super
SUDOKU

Name _____   Date _____

Subtracting With **1, 2, 3,** and **4**

Directions

● Every row, column, and 2-by-2 box ⊞ should contain each of these digits:

1   **2**   **3**   **4**

● Fill in each blank with the correct number to complete the fact.

8 − __ 7	8 − __ 6	7 − 4 __	7 − 3 __
8 − __ 5	6 − 2 __	10 − __ 8	4 − __ 3
13 − __ 9	15 − __ 12	10 − __ 9	4 − 2 __
1__ − 2 10	13 − 2 1__	11 − __ 7	6 − 3 __

Tip!

The answer to a subtraction
problem is called the difference.
What is the difference of 6 and 4?

_____

Name _____ Date _____

Subtracting With 1, 2, 3, and 4

Directions

- Every row, column, and 2-by-2 box ⊞ should contain each of these digits:

  5   6   7   8

- Fill in each blank with the correct number to complete the fact.

$\frac{-\ 3}{4}$	$\begin{array}{r} 9 \\ -\ 4 \\ \hline \end{array}$	$\begin{array}{r} 9 \\ -\ 3 \\ \hline \end{array}$	$\frac{-\ 2}{6}$
$\begin{array}{r} 12 \\ -\ 4 \\ \hline \end{array}$	$\frac{-\ 2}{4}$	$\begin{array}{r} 8 \\ -\ 1 \\ \hline \end{array}$	$\begin{array}{r} 7 \\ -\ 2 \\ \hline \end{array}$
$\frac{1\_}{-\ 4}{11}$	$\frac{-\ 2}{5}$	$\frac{-\ 1}{7}$	$\begin{array}{r} 7 \\ -\ 1 \\ \hline \end{array}$
$\begin{array}{r} 10 \\ -\ 4 \\ \hline \end{array}$	$\begin{array}{r} 10 \\ -\ 2 \\ \hline \end{array}$	$\begin{array}{r} 6 \\ -\ 1 \\ \hline \end{array}$	$\begin{array}{r} 11 \\ -\ 4 \\ \hline \end{array}$

Word Problem

Ray had 10 toy trucks but he lost 2 of them. Then he gave 3 to his little brother. How many does he have left?

_____

Super Sudoku Math: Addition & Subtraction Facts • © 2010 by Eric Charlesworth • Scholastic Teaching Resources

Name _____   Date _____

Subtracting With 1, 2, 3, and 4

Directions

- Every row, column, and 3-by-2 box ▦ should contain each of these digits:

  1   2   3   4   5   6

- Fill in each blank with the correct number to complete the fact.

$\begin{array}{r} \underline{} \\ -\ 3 \\ \hline 2 \end{array}$	$\begin{array}{r} 7 \\ -\ 4 \\ \hline \end{array}$	$\begin{array}{r} 10 \\ -\ 4 \\ \hline \end{array}$	$\begin{array}{r} 10 \\ -\ \underline{} \\ \hline 6 \end{array}$	$\begin{array}{r} 7 \\ -\ \underline{} \\ \hline 6 \end{array}$	$\begin{array}{r} 11 \\ -\ \underline{} \\ \hline 9 \end{array}$
$\begin{array}{r} 8 \\ -\ 4 \\ \hline \end{array}$	$\begin{array}{r} 6 \\ -\ 4 \\ \hline \end{array}$	$\begin{array}{r} 5 \\ -\ 4 \\ \hline \end{array}$	$\begin{array}{r} \underline{} \\ -\ 1 \\ \hline 4 \end{array}$	$\begin{array}{r} 5 \\ -\ 2 \\ \hline \end{array}$	$\begin{array}{r} 9 \\ -\ 3 \\ \hline \end{array}$
$\begin{array}{r} 7 \\ -\ 1 \\ \hline \end{array}$	$\begin{array}{r} 13 \\ -\ 2 \\ \hline 1\_ \end{array}$	$\begin{array}{r} 14 \\ -\ 2 \\ \hline 1 \end{array}$	$\begin{array}{r} 6 \\ -\ 3 \\ \hline \end{array}$	$\begin{array}{r} 14 \\ -\ \underline{} \\ \hline 10 \end{array}$	$\begin{array}{r} 1\_ \\ -\ 3 \\ \hline 12 \end{array}$
$\begin{array}{r} 4 \\ -\ 1 \\ \hline \end{array}$	$\begin{array}{r} 7 \\ -\ 3 \\ \hline \end{array}$	$\begin{array}{r} 1\_ \\ -\ 4 \\ \hline 11 \end{array}$	$\begin{array}{r} \underline{} \\ -\ 2 \\ \hline 4 \end{array}$	$\begin{array}{r} 13 \\ -\ 1 \\ \hline 1\_ \end{array}$	$\begin{array}{r} 1\_ \\ -\ 4 \\ \hline 7 \end{array}$
$\begin{array}{r} 9 \\ -\ \underline{} \\ \hline 7 \end{array}$	$\begin{array}{r} \underline{} \\ -\ 1 \\ \hline 4 \end{array}$	$\begin{array}{r} 1\_ \\ -\ 2 \\ \hline 11 \end{array}$	$\begin{array}{r} 1\_ \\ -\ 3 \\ \hline 8 \end{array}$	$\begin{array}{r} 8 \\ -\ 2 \\ \hline \end{array}$	$\begin{array}{r} 13 \\ -\ \underline{} \\ \hline 9 \end{array}$
$\begin{array}{r} 10 \\ -\ \underline{} \\ \hline 9 \end{array}$	$\begin{array}{r} \underline{} \\ -\ 1 \\ \hline 5 \end{array}$	$\begin{array}{r} 11 \\ -\ \underline{} \\ \hline 7 \end{array}$	$\begin{array}{r} 10 \\ -\ \underline{} \\ \hline 8 \end{array}$	$\begin{array}{r} \underline{} \\ -\ 4 \\ \hline 1 \end{array}$	$\begin{array}{r} \underline{} \\ -\ 2 \\ \hline 1 \end{array}$

Super SUDOKU

SUPER-SIZED!

Name _____ Date _____

Subtracting With **1, 2, 3,** and **4**

Directions

● Every row, column, and 3-by-2 box ⊞ should contain each of these digits:

1 2 3 4 5 6

● Fill in each blank with the correct number to complete the fact.

9 − _ 5	1_ − 3 12	2 − 1 	5 − _ 3	1_ − 3 10	_ − 2 4
6 − 4	8 − 2	7 − 4	_ − 4 1	12 − _ 11	1_ − 3 11
7 − 1	9 − _ 7	1_ − 4 11	_ − 3 0	10 − _ 6	3 − _ 2
5 − 2	3 − 2	11 − _ 7	1_ − 4 12	7 − 2	4 − 2
1_ − 1 10	1_ − 4 9	7 − _ 5	1_ − 2 12	9 − 3	6 − 1
9 − 4	12 − _ 8	_ − 3 3	4 − _ 3	1_ − 3 9	_ − 1 2

Super Sudoku Math: Addition & Subtraction Facts • © 2010 by Eric Charlesworth • Scholastic Teaching Resources

Name _____ Date _____

Subtracting With 5 and 6

Directions

● Every row, column, and 2-by-2 box ⊞ should contain each of these digits:

5   6   7   8

● Fill in each blank with the correct number to complete the fact.

$-\ 5$ $\overline{2}$	13 $-\ 5$ $\overline{}$	6 $-\ \_$ $\overline{1}$	10 $-\ \_$ $\overline{4}$
10 $-\ \_$ $\overline{5}$	15 $-\ \_$ $\overline{9}$	$-\ 5$ $\overline{3}$	12 $-\ 5$ $\overline{}$
9 $-\ \_$ $\overline{3}$	12 $-\ \_$ $\overline{7}$	13 $-\ 6$ $\overline{}$	14 $-\ 6$ $\overline{}$
$-\ 6$ $\overline{2}$	$1\_$ $-\ 6$ $\overline{11}$	$1\_$ $-\ 5$ $\overline{11}$	15 $-\ \_$ $\overline{10}$

Tip!

Subtracting is the opposite (or inverse) of adding. If you add 3 plus 5, you get a sum of 8. That means if you take 5 away from 8, you have a difference 3. So, 3 + 6 = 9 and 9 − 6 = 3.

Super SUDOKU

Name _____ Date _____

Subtracting With **7** and **8**

Directions

● Every row, column, and 2-by-2 box ⊞ should contain each of these digits:

5   6   7   8

● Fill in each blank with the correct number to complete the fact.

9 − __ —— 1	14 − 8 ——	9 − __ —— 2	1__ − 7 —— 8
14 − __ —— 7	13 − 8 ——	15 − __ —— 7	13 − 7 ——
1__ − 8 —— 8	12 − __ —— 5	12 − 7 ——	17 − __ —— 9
1__ − 8 —— 7	19 − __ —— 11	1__ − 7 —— 9	11 − __ —— 4

Word Problem

Ellysa had to water 11 plants. After she had watered 8 of them, how many still needed water?

_____

Super Sudoku Math: Addition & Subtraction Facts • © 2010 by Eric Charlesworth • Scholastic Teaching Resources

Name _____ Date _____

Subtracting With **5, 6, 7,** and **8**

Directions

● Every row, column, and 2-by-2 box ⊞ should contain each of these digits:

1 **2** **3** **4**

● Fill in each blank with the correct number to complete the fact.

7 − 5 ___	11 − 7 ___	9 − 8 ___	1_ − 5 ___ 8
1_ − 6 ___ 5	8 − 5 ___	1_ − 6 ___ 6	10 − 6 ___
1_ − 7 ___ 7	8 − 7 ___	1_ − 8 ___ 5	1_ − 5 ___ 7
10 − 7 ___	10 − 8 ___	1_ − 6 ___ 8	_0 − 5 ___ 5

Word Problem

Liam and his family went on a car trip that was supposed to take 15 hours. After 7 hours, how much time did they have left to drive?

_____

Name _____ Date _____

Subtracting With **5, 6, 7,** and **8**

Directions

● Every row, column, and 2-by-2 box ⊞ should contain each of these digits:

5   6   7   8

● Fill in each blank with the correct number to complete the fact.

14 − __ ‾‾‾ 7	16 − __ ‾‾‾ 8	10 − __ ‾‾‾ 5	12 − __ ‾‾‾ 6
12 − 7 ‾‾‾	1__ − 5 ‾‾‾ 11	1__ − 6 ‾‾‾ 12	1__ − 7 ‾‾‾ 10
11 − 5 ‾‾‾	1__ − 8 ‾‾‾ 7	12 − 5 ‾‾‾	__ − 5 ‾‾‾ 3
15 − 7 ‾‾‾	__ − 5 ‾‾‾ 2	__ − 5 ‾‾‾ 1	11 − 6 ‾‾‾

Tip!

If you are ever subtracting two numbers that are right next to each other you will get the same answer. What answer is it?

_____

Super Sudoku Math: Addition & Subtraction Facts • © 2010 by Eric Charlesworth • Scholastic Teaching Resources

Super SUDOKU

Name _____ Date _____

Subtracting With 1–8

Directions

● Every row, column, and 3-by-2 box ▦ should contain each of these digits:

1 2 3 4 5 6

● Fill in each blank with the correct number to complete the fact.

7 − 6	15 − __ 12	10 − 5	13 − 7	8 − 4	9 − 7
__ − 5 1	12 − 8	1__ − 5 7	11 − 6	9 − 6	1__ − 3 8
11 − 7	8 − 7	10 − __ 7	8 − 6	12 − 6	12 − 7
9 − 4	1__ − 7 5	1__ − 6 10	1__ − 5 9	6 − __ 5	1__ − 5 8
10 − 7	8 − 3	1__ − 7 7	1__ − 8 3	8 − __ 6	10 − 4
10 − 8	14 − 8	1__ − 5 6	1__ − 8 5	7 − __ 2	10 − 6

Super Sudoku Math: Addition & Subtraction Facts • © 2010 by Eric Charlesworth • Scholastic Teaching Resources

35

Name _____   Date _____

Subtracting With 1–8

Directions

● Every row, column, and 3-by-2 box ⊞ should contain each of these digits:

| 1 | 2 | 3 | 4 | 5 | 6 |

● Fill in each blank with the correct number to complete the fact.

8 − __ 6	1_ − 2 9	11 − 5 __	13 − 8 __	10 − 7 __	9 − __ 5
11 − 7 __	10 − __ 5	8 − __ 5	19 − 8 1_	_0 − 8 12	_ − 1 5
13 − __ 10	12 − 6 __	_1 − 8 3	6 − 2 __	9 − 4 __	9 − __ 7
14 − __ 9	7 − 3 __	6 − 4 __	9 − 6 __	_ − 3 3	17 − 6 1_
9 − 8 __	12 − __ 10	16 − __ 11	1_ − 7 9	5 − __ 1	4 − __ 1
13 − 7 __	1_ − 1 12	15 − __ 11	11 − __ 9	16 − 6 _0	7 − 2 __

Super Sudoku Math: Addition & Subtraction Facts • © 2010 by Eric Charlesworth • Scholastic Teaching Resources

Super SUDOKU

Super Sudoku Math: Addition & Subtraction Facts • © 2010 by Eric Charlesworth • Scholastic Teaching Resources

Name _____   Date _____

Subtracting With 9 and 10

Directions

● Every row, column, and 2-by-2 box ⊞ should contain each of these digits:

$$1 \quad 2 \quad 3 \quad 4$$

● Fill in each blank with the correct number to complete the fact.

2_ − 10 —— 12	13 − 9 ——	2_ − 9 —— 12	12 − 9 ——
_6 − 9 —— 7	13 − 10 ——	1_ − 9 —— 3	1_ − 10 —— 4
14 − 10 ——	_8 − 9 —— 9	1_ − 9 —— 4	_0 − 10 —— 10
1_ − 10 —— 3	12 − 10 ——	1_ − 9 —— 5	10 − 9 ——

Tip!

When you subtract by 10, you simply take away 1 from the tens place. You are subtracting 0 from the ones place so it stays the same. What is 54 − 10?

_____

Super SUDOKU

Name _____   Date _____

Subtracting With **11** and **12**

Directions

● Every row, column, and 2-by-2 box ⊞ should contain each of these digits:

1   **2**   **3**   **4**

● Fill in each blank with the correct number to complete the fact.

15 − 12 ────	1_ − 11 ──── 0	1_ − 11 ──── 3	20 − 1_ ──── 8
16 − 12 ────	16 − 1_ ──── 4	2_ − 11 ──── 12	_9 − 12 ──── 7
17 − 1_ ──── 6	2_ − 12 ──── 12	2_ − 11 ──── 11	14 − 11 ────
18 − 1_ ──── 6	1_ − 12 ──── 1	20 − 1_ ──── 9	15 − 11 ────

Word Problem

The bus started with 18 people on it. After 11 people go off at their stops how many people were left on the bus?

_____

Super Sudoku Math: Addition & Subtraction Facts • © 2010 by Eric Charlesworth • Scholastic Teaching Resources

Name _____ Date _____

Subtracting With **9, 10, 11,** and **12**

Directions

● Every row, column, and 2-by-2 box ⊞ should contain each of these digits:

1   2   3   4

● Fill in each blank with the correct number to complete the fact.

15 − 12	14 − 10	2_ − 12 9	11 − 9
12 − 11	12 − 10	12 − 9	1_ − 11 3
1_ − 9 5	10 − 9	2_ − 10 12	1_ − 12 1
1_ − 12 0	1_ − 9 4	15 − 11	2_ − 10 11

Word Problem

Craig was excited because his baseball team won by a score of 13–9. By how many runs did they win?

_____

Super Sudoku Math: Addition & Subtraction Facts • © 2010 by Eric Charlesworth • Scholastic Teaching Resources

Super SUDOKU

Name _____ Date _____

Subtracting With **9, 10, 11,** and **12**

Directions

● Every row, column, and 2-by-2 box ⊞ should contain each of these digits:

5   6   7   8

● Fill in each blank with the correct number to complete the fact.

19 − 12	20 − 12	16 − 11	17 − 11
1_ − 10 ___ 5	16 − 10	1_ − 8 ___ 10	17 − 10
15 − 9	1_ − 9 ___ 6	16 − 9	19 − 11
1_ − 9 ___ 9	18 − 11	18 − 12	17 − 12

Word Problem

Last week Martin had a practice race that was 20 laps long. After he had completed 12 laps, how many did he have left to finish?

_____

Super Sudoku Math: Addition & Subtraction Facts • © 2010 by Eric Charlesworth • Scholastic Teaching Resources

SUPER-SIZED!

Name _____   Date _____

Subtracting With **1–12**

Directions

● Every row, column, and 3-by-2 box ⊞ should contain each of these digits:

1   **2**   **3**   **4**   **5**   **6**

● Fill in each blank with the correct number to complete the fact.

18 − 12	11 − 6	7 − 6	4 − 2	8 − 5	8 − 4
10 − 6	7 − 5	12 − 9	4 − 3	15 − 9	13 − 8
7 − 4	17 − 11	14 − 9	13 − 9	11 − 9	6 − 5
13 − 11	12 − 11	14 − 10	8 − 2	8 − 3	5 − 2
12 − 7	16 − 12	16 − 10	13 − 10	10 − 9	10 − 8
2 − 1	7 − 4	8 − 6	15 − 10	6 − 2	12 − 6

Super SUDOKU

SUPER-SIZED!

Name _____ Date _____

Subtracting With 1–12

Directions

- Every row, column, and 3-by-2 box ▦ should contain each of these digits:

  1 2 3 4 5 6

- Fill in each blank with the correct number to complete the fact.

7 − __ 2	18 − 12	1__ − 12 0	6 − __ 5	1__ − 7 7	11 − 8
__ − 2 2	5 − __ 2	7 − __ 6	7 − __ 5	14 − 9	1__ − 7 9
8 − __ 2	10 − __ 5	11 − __ 7	1__ − 7 6	19 − 1__ 7	10 − __ 9
1__ − 8 4	1__ − 10 1	7 − __ 4	15 − 10	10 − 4	1__ − 12 2
1__ − 6 7	15 − __ 11	6 − __ 1	10 − __ 4	2__ − 10 11	10 − 8
2 − 12 9	16 − 1__ 4	1__ − 8 8	5 − 1	12 − 9	16 − __ 11

42

Super Sudoku Math: Addition & Subtraction Facts • © 2010 by Eric Charlesworth • Scholastic Teaching Resources

Name _____ Date _____

Full Review

Directions

● Every row, column, and 3-by-2 box ⊞ should contain each of these digits:

1 2 3 4 5 6

● Fill in each blank with the correct number to complete the fact.

$\begin{array}{r} 9 \\ + 7 \\ \hline 1\_\ \end{array}$	$\begin{array}{r} 9 \\ + 4 \\ \hline 1\_\ \end{array}$	$\begin{array}{r} 8 \\ + 7 \\ \hline 1\_\ \end{array}$	$\begin{array}{r} 6 \\ + 7 \\ \hline \_3 \end{array}$	$\begin{array}{r} \_ \\ + 6 \\ \hline 8 \end{array}$	$\begin{array}{r} \_ \\ + 4 \\ \hline 8 \end{array}$
$\begin{array}{r} 9 \\ - 7 \\ \hline \end{array}$	$\begin{array}{r} 5 \\ - 4 \\ \hline \end{array}$	$\begin{array}{r} 10 \\ - 6 \\ \hline \end{array}$	$\begin{array}{r} 10 \\ - 4 \\ \hline \end{array}$	$\begin{array}{r} 1\_ \\ - 10 \\ \hline 3 \end{array}$	$\begin{array}{r} 11 \\ - 6 \\ \hline \end{array}$
$\begin{array}{r} 2 \\ + 1 \\ \hline \end{array}$	$\begin{array}{r} 12 \\ +12 \\ \hline 2\_\ \end{array}$	$\begin{array}{r} 12 \\ + \_ \\ \hline 18 \end{array}$	$\begin{array}{r} 10 \\ + 5 \\ \hline 1\_\ \end{array}$	$\begin{array}{r} 6 \\ + 5 \\ \hline 1\_\ \end{array}$	$\begin{array}{r} 6 \\ + 6 \\ \hline 1\_\ \end{array}$
$\begin{array}{r} 12 \\ - 11 \\ \hline \end{array}$	$\begin{array}{r} 12 \\ - 7 \\ \hline \end{array}$	$\begin{array}{r} 12 \\ - 10 \\ \hline \end{array}$	$\begin{array}{r} 12 \\ - 9 \\ \hline \end{array}$	$\begin{array}{r} 12 \\ - 8 \\ \hline \end{array}$	$\begin{array}{r} 12 \\ - 6 \\ \hline \end{array}$
$\begin{array}{r} 2 \\ + 2 \\ \hline \end{array}$	$\begin{array}{r} 8 \\ + 8 \\ \hline 1\_\ \end{array}$	$\begin{array}{r} 8 \\ + \_ \\ \hline 11 \end{array}$	$\begin{array}{r} 1 \\ + 1 \\ \hline \end{array}$	$\begin{array}{r} 11 \\ + 4 \\ \hline 1\_\ \end{array}$	$\begin{array}{r} 4 \\ + 6 \\ \hline \_0 \end{array}$
$\begin{array}{r} 12 \\ - 7 \\ \hline \end{array}$	$\begin{array}{r} 5 \\ - 3 \\ \hline \end{array}$	$\begin{array}{r} 7 \\ - 6 \\ \hline \end{array}$	$\begin{array}{r} 12 \\ - 8 \\ \hline \end{array}$	$\begin{array}{r} 17 \\ - 11 \\ \hline \end{array}$	$\begin{array}{r} 10 \\ - \_ \\ \hline 7 \end{array}$

Name _____ Date _____

Full Review

Directions

● Every row, column, and 3-by-2 box ⊞ should contain each of these digits:

1   2   3   4   5   6

● Fill in each blank with the correct number to complete the fact.

9 $+\ \_$ $\overline{15}$	7 $+\ \_$ $\overline{10}$	12 $+\ \_$ $\overline{17}$	7 $+\ \_$ $\overline{8}$	10 $+\ \_$ $\overline{12}$	12 $+\ \_$ $\overline{16}$
$1\_$ $+\ 3$ $\overline{15}$	6 $+1\_$ $\overline{17}$	10 $+\ \_$ $\overline{14}$	8 $+\ 8$ $\overline{1\_}$	11 $+\ 2$ $\overline{1\_}$	5 $+10$ $\overline{1\_}$
12 $+11$ $\overline{2\_}$	2 $+\ 2$ $\overline{\ }$	5 $+\ 1$ $\overline{\ }$	7 $+\ 8$ $\overline{1\_}$	9 $+\ 2$ $\overline{1\_}$	6 $+\ 6$ $\overline{1\_}$
7 $-\ 6$ $\overline{\ }$	13 $-\ 8$ $\overline{\ }$	14 -12 $\overline{\ }$	14 -11 $\overline{\ }$	6 $-\ 2$ $\overline{\ }$	11 $-\ 5$ $\overline{\ }$
$1\_$ $-\ 8$ $\overline{6}$	$1\_$ $-\ 8$ $\overline{8}$	10 $-\ 7$ $\overline{\ }$	9 -7 $\overline{\ }$	6 -1 $\overline{\ }$	4 $-\ \_$ $\overline{3}$
14 $-\ \_$ $\overline{9}$	$1\_$ $-\ 1$ $\overline{11}$	5 $-\ \_$ $\overline{4}$	15 -11 $\overline{\ }$	13 $-\ 7$ $\overline{\ }$	7 -4 $\overline{\ }$

Super Sudoku Math: Addition & Subtraction Facts • © 2010 by Eric Charlesworth • Scholastic Teaching Resources

Super SUDOKU

Name _____ Date _____

Full Review

Directions

● Every row, column, and 3-by-2 box ⊞ should contain each of these digits:

1 2 3 4 5 6

● Fill in each blank with the correct number to complete the fact.

$\begin{array}{r} \_\_ \\ +\ 7 \\ \hline 13 \end{array}$	$\begin{array}{r} 8 \\ +\ 3 \\ \hline 1\_ \end{array}$	$\begin{array}{r} 12 \\ +12 \\ \hline 2\_ \end{array}$	$\begin{array}{r} 5 \\ -\ 2 \\ \hline \end{array}$	$\begin{array}{r} 9 \\ -\ 4 \\ \hline \end{array}$	$\begin{array}{r} 7 \\ -\ 5 \\ \hline \end{array}$
$\begin{array}{r} 8 \\ +\ \_ \\ \hline 10 \end{array}$	$\begin{array}{r} 12 \\ +\ 3 \\ \hline 1\_ \end{array}$	$\begin{array}{r} 8 \\ +\ 5 \\ \hline 1\_ \end{array}$	$\begin{array}{r} 15 \\ -\ 9 \\ \hline \end{array}$	$\begin{array}{r} 9 \\ -\ 5 \\ \hline \end{array}$	$\begin{array}{r} 2 \\ -\ 1 \\ \hline \end{array}$
$\begin{array}{r} 11 \\ +\ \_ \\ \hline 14 \end{array}$	$\begin{array}{r} 7 \\ +\ \_ \\ \hline 9 \end{array}$	$\begin{array}{r} 6 \\ +\ 9 \\ \hline 1\_ \end{array}$	$\begin{array}{r} 12 \\ -11 \\ \hline \end{array}$	$\begin{array}{r} 1\_ \\ -\ 4 \\ \hline 12 \end{array}$	$\begin{array}{r} 15 \\ -11 \\ \hline \end{array}$
$\begin{array}{r} 8 \\ +1\_ \\ \hline 19 \end{array}$	$\begin{array}{r} 4 \\ +\ \_ \\ \hline 8 \end{array}$	$\begin{array}{r} 2 \\ +\ \_ \\ \hline 8 \end{array}$	$\begin{array}{r} 4 \\ -\ 2 \\ \hline \end{array}$	$\begin{array}{r} 13 \\ -10 \\ \hline \end{array}$	$\begin{array}{r} 11 \\ -\ 6 \\ \hline \end{array}$
$\begin{array}{r} 2 \\ +\ 3 \\ \hline \end{array}$	$\begin{array}{r} 3 \\ +\ \_ \\ \hline 6 \end{array}$	$\begin{array}{r} 7 \\ +\ 4 \\ \hline 1\_ \end{array}$	$\begin{array}{r} 1\_ \\ -\ 5 \\ \hline 9 \end{array}$	$\begin{array}{r} 12 \\ -10 \\ \hline \end{array}$	$\begin{array}{r} \_\_ \\ -\ 1 \\ \hline 5 \end{array}$
$\begin{array}{r} 7 \\ +\ 7 \\ \hline 1\_ \end{array}$	$\begin{array}{r} 6 \\ +\ \_ \\ \hline 12 \end{array}$	$\begin{array}{r} 1 \\ +\ 1 \\ \hline \end{array}$	$\begin{array}{r} 1\_ \\ -\ 4 \\ \hline 11 \end{array}$	$\begin{array}{r} 11 \\ -\ \_ \\ \hline 10 \end{array}$	$\begin{array}{r} 4 \\ -\ \_ \\ \hline 1 \end{array}$

Name _____ Date _____

Full Review

Directions

● Every row, column, and 3-by-2 box ⊞ should contain each of these digits:

1 2 3 4 5 6

● Fill in each blank with the correct number to complete the fact.

6 + 7 ――― 1_	13 − 7 ――― 	7 + 5 ――― 1_	15 − _ ――― 11	6 + 1_ ――― 17	7 − 2 ―――
5 + 6 ――― 1_	8 − 4 ――― 	7 + 8 ――― 1_	2_ − 12 ――― 10	10 + _ ――― 16	14 − 11 ―――
8 +12 ――― _0	14 − 9 ――― 	9 +12 ――― 2_	18 − 12 ――― 	9 + _ ――― 12	15 − 11 ―――
12 +12 ――― 2_	8 − _ ――― 5	3 + 3 ――― 	11 − 6 ――― 	5 + 1_ ――― 17	10 − 9 ―――
4 + 2 ――― 	8 − _ ――― 7	1 + 3 ――― 	8 − 5 ――― 	9 + 6 ――― 1_	8 − 6 ―――
7 + _ ――― 12	11 − _ ――― 9	10 + 3 ――― 1_	4 − 3 ――― 	7 + 7 ――― 1_	1_ − 7 ――― 9

Super Sudoku Math: Addition & Subtraction Facts • © 2010 by Eric Charlesworth • Scholastic Teaching Resources

Super SUDOKU

Name _____ Date _____

Full Review

Directions

● Every row, column, and 3-by-2 box ⊞ should contain each of these digits:

| 1 | 2 | 3 | 4 | 5 | 6 |

● Fill in each blank with the correct number to complete the fact.

4 + 2	9 − 5	9 + 3 —— 1_	16 − _ —— 11	3 + _ —— 4	_ − 3 —— 0
11 − _ —— 6	6 + 7 —— 1_	2_ − 10 —— 11	9 + 5 —— 1_	1_ − 9 —— 7	11 + 1 —— 1_
0 + 2	8 − _ —— 2	9 + 4 —— 1_	2_ − 9 —— 12	7 + 7 —— 1_	1_ − 4 —— 11
10 − 6	_ + 7 —— 8	6 − 1	_ + 7 —— 9	1_ − 2 —— 11	4 + _ —— 10
12 + 1 —— 1_	9 − 7	3 + _ —— 7	17 − 11	5 + _ —— 10	1_ − 7 —— 4
10 − 9	2 + 3	16 − 10	_ + 8 —— 11	20 − 8 —— 1_	_ + 6 —— 10

Answer Key

Page 7

5	7	8	6
6	8	5	7
7	5	6	8
8	6	7	5

Page 8

4	2	1	3
1	3	4	2
3	1	2	4
2	4	3	1

Page 9

1	2	4	3
3	4	2	1
2	3	1	4
4	1	3	2

Tip: 7

Page 10

7	5	6	8
6	8	7	5
5	6	8	7
8	7	5	6

Word Problem: 12 pens

Page 11

2	4	3	1	5	6
5	1	6	3	2	4
3	2	1	4	6	5
4	6	5	2	3	1
6	3	4	5	1	2
1	5	2	6	4	3

Page 12

6	5	3	4	1	2
1	2	4	5	6	3
3	4	5	6	2	1
2	1	6	3	4	5
4	3	2	1	5	6
5	6	1	2	3	4

Page 13

6	7	8	5
5	8	7	6
7	5	6	8
8	6	5	7

Page 14

7	8	5	6
5	6	8	7
6	5	7	8
8	7	6	5

Word Problem: 17 pages

Page 15

1	2	4	3
3	4	2	1
2	3	1	4
4	1	3	2

Word Problem: 13 pieces

Page 16

7	5	6	8
6	8	7	5
5	6	8	7
8	7	5	6

Word Problem: Yes. They have 11 dollars.

Page 17

3	2	4	6	1	5
6	5	1	3	4	2
2	4	6	5	3	1
1	3	5	2	6	4
5	1	3	4	2	6
4	6	2	1	5	3

Page 18

3	1	4	6	2	5
2	5	6	4	3	1
1	6	2	5	4	3
4	3	5	2	1	6
5	4	1	3	6	2
6	2	3	1	5	4

Page 19

7	5	6	8
8	6	7	5
5	7	8	6
6	8	5	7

Tip: 86

Page 20

1	3	4	2
2	4	1	3
3	1	2	4
4	2	3	1

Word Problem: 21 fireflies

Page 21

1	3	4	2
2	4	1	3
3	1	2	4
4	2	3	1

Page 22

7	8	6	5
5	6	8	7
8	5	7	6
6	7	5	8

Word Problem: 22 blocks

Page 23

5	2	3	4	1	6
6	1	4	3	5	2
3	5	2	1	6	4
4	6	1	2	3	5
2	3	6	5	4	1
1	4	5	6	2	3

Page 24

2	4	5	6	1	3
3	6	1	4	2	5
4	5	2	1	3	6
6	1	3	5	4	2
5	2	4	3	6	1
1	3	6	2	5	4

Page 25

3	4	1	2
1	2	4	3
2	1	3	4
4	3	2	1

Page 26

1	2	3	4
3	4	2	1
4	3	1	2
2	1	4	3

Word Problem: 12 grapes